SCIENCE GENERAL

Reading Level: 3–4
Interest Level: 3–6

Complete Set of 6 Library books:
$169.62/**$127.20**
ISBN: 9781538289211
Individual Titles: $28.27/**$21.20**

Specs: 32 pp., 8 ½" x 11", Full-Color Photographs, Graphic Organizers

- Engages reluctant readers with high-interest content
- Supports elementary science curricula
- Graphic organizers enhance reader comprehension

Extreme Science

"Extreme" means to a very great degree. An extreme material could be the rarest there is. The deep ocean is an extreme habitat. Even gravity can be an extreme force! In this set, readers learn about extreme qualities and experiences, and how things have evolved and adapted to reach their extreme state. The main text looks at how we can gather scientific information from these extreme states, forces, materials, plants, and other living things. Presented in a highly accessible way, Extreme Science appeals to visual learners with its awesome design and graphics.

	Library Bound Book			
① Awesome Matter and Materials Dewey: • GRL: P • ATOS: PENDING	9781538288825	GS7791	①	©2024
② Incredible Living Things Dewey: • GRL: P • ATOS: PENDING	9781538288764	GS7792	②	©2024
③ Magnificent Habitats Dewey: • GRL: P • ATOS: PENDING	9781538288795	GS7793	③	©2024
④ Phenomenal Plants Dewey: • GRL: P • ATOS: PENDING	9781538288856	GS7794	④	©2024
⑤ Powerful Forces Dewey: • GRL: P • ATOS: PENDING	9781538288887	GS7795	⑤	©2024
⑥ Spectacular Light and Sound Dewey: • GRL: P • ATOS: PENDING	9781538288917	GS7796	⑥	©2024

 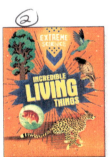  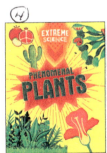  

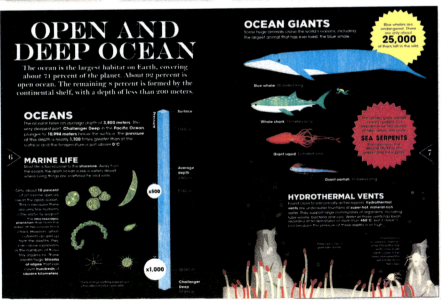

Extreme Science

MAGNIFICENT HABITATS

Rob Colson and Jon Richards

Please visit our website, www.garethstevens.com. For a free color catalog of all our high-quality books, call toll free 1-800-542-2595 or fax 1-877-542-2596.

Cataloging-in-Publication Data

Names: Colson, Rob. | Richards, Jon.
Title: Magnificent habitats / by Rob Colson and Jon Richards.
Description: New York : Gareth Stevens Publishing, 2024. | Series: Extreme science | Includes glossary and index.
Identifiers: ISBN 9781538288788 (pbk.) | ISBN 9781538288795 (library bound) | ISBN 9781538288801 (ebook)
Subjects: LCSH: Habitat (Ecology)--Juvenile literature.
Classification: LCC QH541.14 C563 2024 | DDC 577--dc23

Published in 2024 by
Gareth Stevens Publishing
2544 Clinton St.
Buffalo, NY 14224

Editor: Amy Pimperton
Text written by Rob Colson and Jon Richards
Produced by Tall Tree Ltd
Designers: Malcolm Parchment and Ben Ruocco

Picture credits:
Every attempt has been made to clear copyright. Should there be any inadvertant omission, please apply to the publisher for rectification.

First published in Great Britain in 2019 by Wayland Copyright © Hodder and Stoughton, 2019

All rights reserved. No part of this book may be reproduced in any form without permission in writing from the publisher, except by a reviewer.

Printed in the United States of America

CPSIA compliance information: Batch #CSGS24: For further information contact Gareth Stevens at 1-800-542-2595.

Find us on

CONTENTS

A WORLD OF HABITATS 4
OPEN AND DEEP OCEAN 6
COASTAL HABITATS 8
CORAL REEFS 10
NORTHERN FORESTS 12
TEMPERATE FORESTS 14
RAIN FORESTS 16
TEMPERATE GRASSLANDS 18
TROPICAL GRASSLANDS 20
RIVERS AND WETLANDS 22
DESERTS 24
MOUNTAINS 26
TUNDRA AND THE POLES 28
GLOSSARY 30
INDEX 32

A WORLD OF HABITATS

Earth is covered in a rich variety of habitats. Each habitat is a different type of environment in which different organisms live. These range from the cold, icy regions around the poles to the scorching deserts at the equator and down to the depths of the ocean floor.

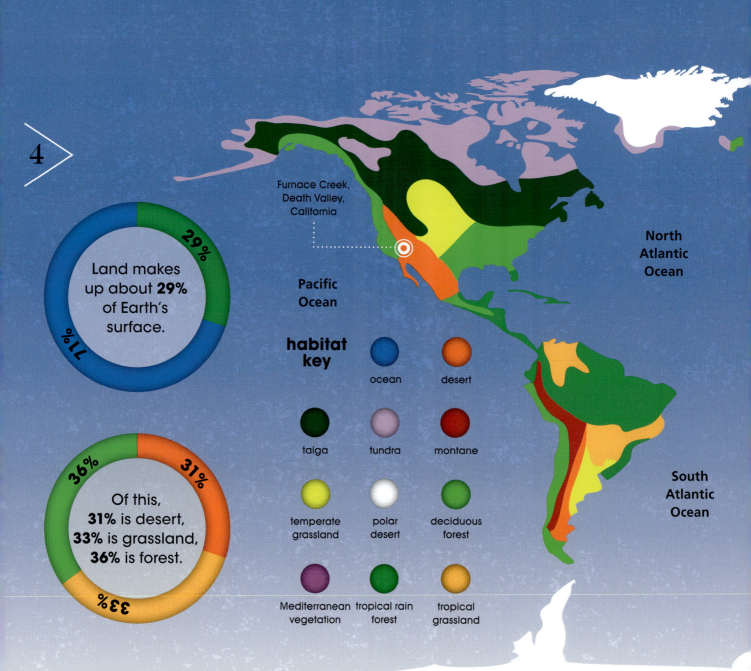

Land makes up about **29%** of Earth's surface. **71%** / **29%**

Of this, **31%** is desert, **33%** is grassland, **36%** is forest.

habitat key
- ocean
- desert
- taiga
- tundra
- montane
- temperate grassland
- polar desert
- deciduous forest
- Mediterranean vegetation
- tropical rain forest
- tropical grassland

Furnace Creek, Death Valley, California

Pacific Ocean

North Atlantic Ocean

South Atlantic Ocean

EXTREMES ON EARTH

HOTTEST PLACE

The highest temperature ever recorded is **135.6°F (57.6°C)**, at **Furnace Creek** in **Death Valley, California**. The **Mojave fringe-toed lizard** lives there. When temperatures become too hot, the lizard "swims" under the sand to find cooler conditions.

The fringe-toed lizard has triangular fringes on its toes to stop it from sinking into the sand when it runs.

In the McMurdo Dry Valleys of Antarctica **NO RAIN OR SNOW** has fallen for nearly 2 million years.

COLDEST PLACE

The lowest temperature ever recorded is **-128.6°F (-89.2°C)**, at **Vostok Station, Antarctica**. Vostok Station is also one of the sunniest places on Earth, with nearly **4,000 hours** of sunshine **per year**.

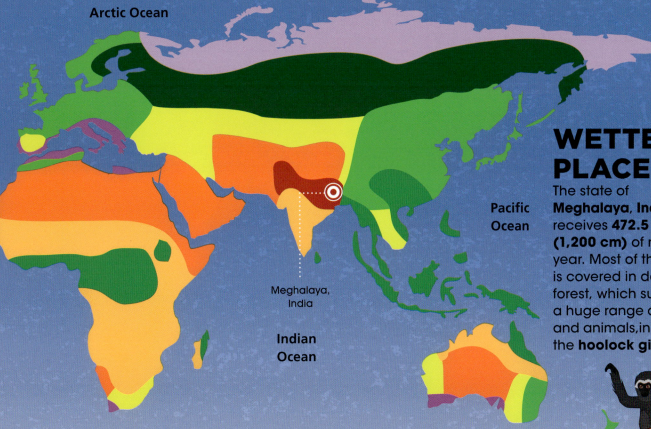

WETTEST PLACE

The state of **Meghalaya, India**, receives **472.5 inches (1,200 cm)** of rain per year. Most of the state is covered in dense forest, which supports a huge range of plants and animals, including the **hoolock gibbon**.

Hoolock gibbons spend most of their lives in trees. Males are black and females are brown.

OPEN AND DEEP OCEAN

The ocean is the largest habitat on Earth, covering about 71 percent of the planet. About 92 percent is open ocean. The other 8 percent is the continental shelf, with a depth of less than 600 feet (200 m).

OCEANS

The oceans have an average depth of about **12,470 feet (3,800 m)**. The very deepest part, **Challenger Deep** in the **Pacific Ocean**, plunges to **36,070 feet (10,994 m)** below the surface. The **pressure** at this depth is nearly **1,100** times greater than at the surface and the temperature is just above **32°F (0°C)**.

MARINE LIFE

Most life is found close to the **shoreline**. Away from the coasts the open ocean is like a watery desert, where living things are scattered far and wide.

Only about **10 percent** of all marine species live in the open ocean. This is because there are very few nutrients in the water to support the **microscopic plankton** that form the basis of the ocean food chain. However, when nutrients do well up from the depths, they can cause explosions in the numbers of these tiny organisms. These create huge **blooms of algae** that can cover **thousands** of **square miles**.

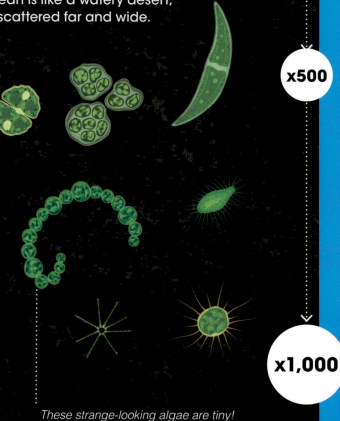

These strange-looking algae are tiny!

Pressure

- surface
- 3,280 feet (1,000 m)
- **average depth** 12,470 feet (3,800 m)
- x500
- 16,400 feet (5,000 m)
- x1,000
- 32,800 feet (10,000 m)
- **Challenger Deep** 36,070 feet (10,994 m)

OCEAN GIANTS

Some huge animals cruise the world's oceans, including the largest animal that has ever lived, the blue whale.

Blue whales are endangered. There are only about **25,000** of them left in the wild.

blue whale: 100 feet (30 m) long

whale shark: 43 feet (13 m) long

giant squid: 40 feet (12 m) long

The solitary giant oarfish is rarely spotted. It is thought to be the source of tales about fearsome **SEA SERPENTS** that appear in the ancient myths of the Greeks and the Vikings.

giant oarfish: 36 feet (11 m) long

HYDROTHERMAL VENTS

Found close to volcanically active regions, **hydrothermal vents** are underwater fountains of **super-hot, mineral-rich** water. They support large communities of organisms, including tube worms, bacteria, and eels. Water at these vents has been recorded at temperatures of more than **840°F (450°C)**, but it doesn't boil because the pressure at these depths is so high.

Riftia pachyptila, or giant tube worms

Kiwa hirsuta is a crustacean that lives around hydrothermal vents in the South Pacific Ocean. It has been nicknamed the yeti lobster for its hairy legs.

COASTAL HABITATS

Close to land, conditions change regularly as the tide moves up and down the shore and where rivers flow into the sea, carrying fresh water and huge amounts of sediment. These regions are teeming with life as ocean currents bring nutrients to create a rich habitat.

HIGH TIDE

Gravitational forces from the sun and moon pull on the waters of the ocean, causing the tides to rise and fall each day. The greatest tidal range is found at the **Bay of Fundy** in Canada, where the waters rise and fall by as much as **50 feet (15 m)** with each tide. That's the average height of a four-story building.

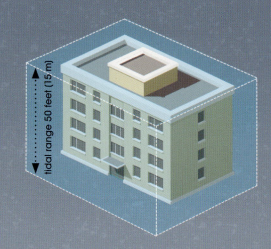

ROCK POOLS

At low tide, pools form in rocks on the shore. These shallow rock pools provide a refuge for creatures to survive until high tide. Creatures you might find in a rock pool include **starfish, sea anemones,** and **hermit crabs.** Starfish and sea anemones are animals with no **brain, heart,** or **blood.**

Sea anemones have stinging tentacles that they use to catch tiny plankton.

When they eat, **starfish** can eject their stomachs out of their bodies to collect food, which they then suck back in.

Hermit crabs live inside shells that they find on the seabed.

TOUGH TEETH

Limpets are shellfish that feed by scouring rocks. A limpet's **teeth** are the strongest known biological substance and are capable of scraping off pieces of rock.

At low tide, limpets cling tightly to rocks. This stops the limpets from drying out.

On a beach, buried beneath every 10 square feet (1 sq m) of sand, there may be as many as **2,000 SHELLFISH** hiding in burrows, waiting for the tide to return.

OCEAN MEADOWS

The nutrients in coastal regions lead to the growth of several rich habitats, such as **kelp forests** and **seagrass meadows**. These places support a wide range of plant and animal life and protect coastal areas from **erosion**.

Some species of kelp can grow up to **24 inches (60 cm)** in a single day!

giant kelp: up to 100 feet (30 m)

manatee

Manatees are large mammals that graze on seagrass in tropical coastal waters. They can grow up to **13 FEET (4 M) LONG.**

VAST GRASS

Seagrass meadows are thought to make up about **15 percent** of the ocean's ability to store carbon.

SALTY FORESTS

Mangrove swamps are coastal habitats where plants and animals have evolved to cope with the salty conditions, which can be more than twice as salty as normal seawater.

Mudskippers are **amphibious fish** that live in mangrove swamps. They can walk on land by **pulling** themselves along with their fins.

CORAL REEFS

Coral reefs are some of the richest habitats on the planet. They support at least 25 percent of all sea species and can stretch for thousands of miles. These huge structures are formed from the dead bodies of tiny creatures.

TINY BUILDERS

Coral reefs are built by colonies of tiny organisms called **coral polyps**. These polyps form a hard outer **exoskeleton** for protection. When the polyp dies, the exoskeleton remains and more polyps grow on top of it. Over thousands of years, the exoskeletons build up to form a **reef**.

coral polyp

GREAT BARRIER REEF

The **Great Barrier Reef** off the north-east coast of Australia is the largest coral reef in the world, stretching for about **1,430 miles (2,300 km)**. It started to form about **6,000** years ago and is home to about **9,000** marine species:

- 6 species of **marine turtles**
- 30 species of **marine mammals**
- 100 species of **jellyfish**
- 215 species of **birds**
- 133 species of **rays** and **sharks**
- 500 species of **worms**
- 1,300 species of **crustaceans**
- 1,625 species of **fish**
- 2,000 species of **sponges**
- 3,000+ species of **mollusks**.

THE GREAT BARRIER REEF IS THE ONLY LIVING STRUCTURE VISIBLE FROM **SPACE.**

BARRIER REEF LIFE

Gulls nest on nearby land, and come to the reef to catch fish.

Rays stay close to the ocean floor as they feed.

Dolphins visit the reef to feed on the many fish found there.

Jellyfish are attracted to the warm tropical water.

WRASSE CHANGE!

The **humphead wrasse** is a large fish found in coral reefs. Some **female** wrasse can change into males when they are around **9 years** old. The males grow up to **6.5 feet (2 m)** long, twice as long as the females, and have even bigger humps on their heads.

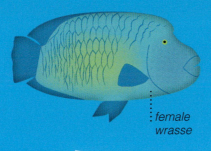

male wrasse

female wrasse

THE HUMPHEAD WRASSE IS ALSO KNOWN AS THE **NAPOLEON WRASSE.**

ANNUAL FEAST

Every year, the corals release huge clouds of **eggs** and **sperm** in a mass **spawning** event. This attracts a huge amount of wildlife that feed off the eggs, including the biggest fish in the sea, the **whale shark**.

whale shark

coral eggs

Coral reefs are under threat from **rising** sea temperatures, caused by global warming. This **bleaches** the coral and may even kill it. According to some studies, up to **60 percent** of the world's coral reefs are under threat from climate change caused by humans.

bleached coral

11

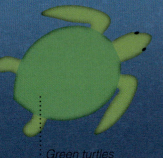

Turtles come to the Barrier Reef to mate and nest.

Green turtles feed on seagrass.

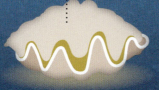

Giant clams can live for more than 100 years.

Clams stay in one place and feed on passing plankton.

Sponges are simple brainless animals that feed by allowing water to flow through them.

fan worm

Bristle worms are predators on the ocean floor.

Sea worms on the reef come in many shapes, sizes and colors.

NORTHERN FORESTS

Stretching right across the northern parts of Asia, Europe, and North America is an enormous band of forest. Known as taiga or boreal forest, it makes up the largest habitat on land and accounts for as much as 29 percent of Earth's forests.

HARSH CONDITIONS

Conditions in **boreal forests** can be very harsh, with long, cold winters and short summers.

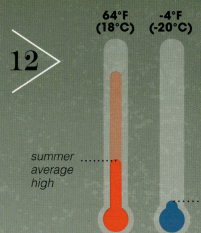

64°F (18°C)   -4°F (-20°C)

summer average high

winter average high

TEMPERATURE RANGE

It can be warm in the brief summer, sometimes reaching **86°F (30°C)**, but temperatures plunge below **-58°F (-50°C)** in winter.

The growing season is very short and can last as little as **50 DAYS** in some areas.

In the depths of winter, daylight can last for just **5 hours**.

sun rising at 9.30 a.m. and setting at 2.30 p.m.

TOUGH TREES

Evergreen trees dominate the forests. They have **thin, needle-like** leaves that are tough enough to survive the cold conditions and **reduce** water loss. The leaves stay on **all year round** so that the tree can make enough food during the short winter days to survive.

The needles on fir trees are attached to the branches in clusters.

SURVIVING THE EXTREMES

Animals that live in these cold regions have special **adaptations** to **survive** when conditions get tough.

The caribou is known in Europe as the **REINDEER**. In northern Finland, the Sami people survive by migrating with their herds of reindeer.

Caribou grow thick, woolly fur in winter. The fur thins out during the summer.

Caribou hooves are wide to stop the animals from sinking into the snow. They have sharp edges to help grip ice and rocks.

wolf

13

MIGRATING HERDS

Porcupine caribou take part in the longest land animal migration in North America. Huge herds of more than **200,000** animals walk more than **1,490 miles (2,400 km)** each year across northern Canada and Alaska.

Wolves hunt large prey, such as caribou, by working together in packs. Like their prey, the wolves' winter fur keeps them warm even when temperatures drop to **-40°F (-40°C)**.

HIBERNATION

Some animals **hibernate** during the winter months, slowing down their metabolism (the rate their bodies work at) to preserve energy. Brown bears eat as much as they can in summer. During their winter hibernation, they lose about half their body weight.

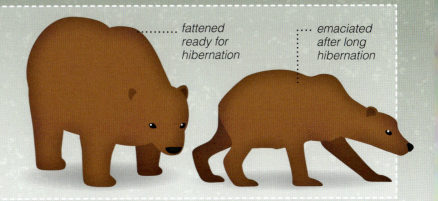

fattened ready for hibernation

emaciated after long hibernation

TEMPERATE FORESTS

Further away from the poles than boreal forests, temperate forests are found in the world's temperate regions, where conditions are milder.

beech
deciduous

pine
evergreen

FOUR SEASONS

Warmer winters, four distinct seasons and regular rainfall mean that temperate forests can include a mixture of **deciduous** and **evergreen** trees.

MILD AND WET

The temperature range is narrow. Rainfall measures between **30 to 60 inches (75 to 150 cm)** per year.

While **evergreen** trees keep their leaves all year round, **deciduous** trees lose their leaves each year. In autumn, the green **chlorophyll** in their leaves breaks down. The leaves turn from green into a range of browns, reds, oranges, and yellows, before falling off.

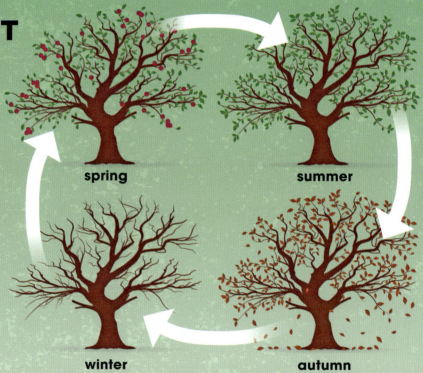

spring — summer — autumn — winter

In autumn, fallen leaves cover the forest floor, creating a layer called **leaf litter**. As it **rots**, it releases nutrients into the soil.

Leaf litter is also a source of food for **slugs**, **snails**, **woodlice**, **beetles**, and other **bugs**.

RAIN FORESTS

These lush habitats are found in wet parts of the world, both in the tropics and in temperate regions. A huge variety of plants and animals live here. They have adapted to the warm and wet conditions.

TROPICAL RAIN FORESTS

Tropical rain forests cover just 6 percent of Earth's land surface, but the plants growing there produce about 28 percent of the world's oxygen by photosynthesis.

Out of more than 10 million species of plants and animals that have been identified by scientists on Earth, more than half of them live in tropical rain forests.

LAYERED LIFE
Plants in the rain forest grow in four distinct layers.

emergents: The tallest poke out of the top of the canopy, reaching up to 230 feet (70 m).

canopy: This is the main tree level in a rain forest, forming a continuous layer of foliage that reaches about 164 feet (50 m).

under canopy: This is made up of smaller trees.

A **raindrop** can take **10 minutes** to drip from the thick canopy to the forest floor.

shrub and forest floor: With very little light, only small, short plants are found here.

VAST AMAZON

The **Amazon Rain Forest** in South America covers a vast area. It is so big that, if it were a separate country, it would be the **seventh** biggest in the world. Bigger than the whole of **India**.

Amazon Rain Forest

India

GROWING ON TREES

Rain forest plants called **epiphytes**, such as **orchids**, do not grow on the ground. Instead, they grow out of trees.

PLANTS

The Teresensis' bromeliad treefrog lays its eggs in pools that form inside the leaves of bromeliad plants. The **tadpoles** hatch and grow into adult frogs before leaving the pool.

tadpoles

Bromeliads are a large group of plants that includes the pineapple.

SHRINKING FORESTS

Rain forests are cleared to make room for human **settlements**, **mines**, **farms**, and **plantations**. An area the size of a **soccer field** is cleared every single second. **Twenty percent** of the Amazon Rain Forest has already disappeared.

AN AREA THE SIZE OF THE STATE OF NEW JERSEY DISAPPEARS EVERY YEAR.

TEMPERATE RAIN FORESTS

These are found in **cooler** parts of the world, such as **North America**, **East Asia**, and **Australia**. Temperate rain forests have two distinct seasons: a **wet** season and a **dry** season. Some of the largest living things on the planet are found here. **Giant redwoods** in California can grow to more than **328 feet (100 m)** in height, or taller than the **Statue of Liberty**.

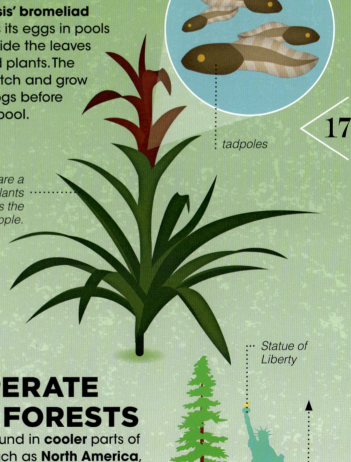

Statue of Liberty

305 feet (92.99 m)

17

TEMPERATE GRASSLANDS

All of the world's continents, except for Antarctica, have large areas of grassland. Temperate grassland regions are found in cooler areas away from the tropics. These vast habitats are home to enormous groups of animals.

SEASONS

Temperate grasslands experience **four** seasons each year (**spring, summer, autumn,** and **winter**) with temperatures ranging from **14°F (-10°C)** in winter to **82°F (28°C)** in summer. They usually receive between **12 to 24 inches (30 to 60 cm)** of rain a year.

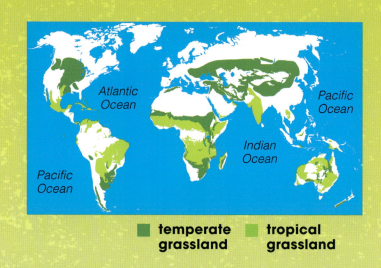

■ temperate grassland   ■ tropical grassland

MANY NAMES
Temperate grasslands have different names around the world:

NORTH AMERICA	SOUTH AMERICA	CENTRAL EUROPE AND ASIA
PRAIRIES	**PAMPAS**	**STEPPE**

Subsoil is a mixture of sand and clay under the roots.

Roots take water and minerals from the soil.

Some grasses grow to **23 feet (7 m) tall** and send roots down **6.5 feet (2 m)** to find moisture.

CLEVER CRITTERS

Prairie dogs are **rodents** that live in huge **underground burrows** called towns. The biggest town ever found was in **Texas**. It covered about **16 million acres (65,000 sq km)** and was home to about **400 million prairie dogs**.

Prairie dogs warn each other when predators approach. They have **different** calls for different predators, such as **coyotes**, **eagles**, or even **humans**. They also describe the **size** and **color** of the predator, so their call for a human in a **red** T-shirt will be different from their call for a human in a **blue** T-shirt.

16 MILLION ACRES IS AN AREA THE SIZE OF THE STATE OF **WEST VIRGINIA**.

Prairie dogs are a type of **GROUND SQUIRREL** found in the United States, Canada, and Mexico.

One dog barks a warning.

Prairie dogs watch vigilantly.

potential threat

In the United States, the bison is also known as the **BUFFALO**.

Bison roam in separate herds of males and females.

DISAPPEARING BISON

The prairies once supported huge herds of **bison**. There were **tens of millions** of them at the start of the **1800s**. During the next **100 years**, hunters killed an estimated **50 million** bison, reducing their numbers to fewer than **1,000** throughout the whole of **North America** by **1889**. Today, they have recovered to about **200,000**.

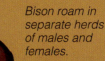

Wildfires are important in grassland areas. They stop large trees from growing, but grasses can grow back because, unlike many other plants, they grow from their **bases** or even parts that lie below the soil. Fire may destroy the top of the grass, but the growing part survives and the grass regrows.

Wildfires spread swiftly in dry summers.

TROPICAL GRASSLANDS

Tropical grasslands cover huge areas of Africa and are also found in India, Nepal, Australia, and parts of the Americas. Warmer than temperate grasslands, they also receive a lot more rainfall.

WET AND DRY

Temperatures range from **60°F to 95°F (15°C to 35°C)** and the grasslands can receive up to **60 inches (150 cm)** of rain a year. There are two seasons each year: a **wet season** when rainfall is high and a **dry season** when the rains stop.

20

SERENGETI

The Serengeti in **Tanzania** and **Kenya** in East Africa is one of the richest grassland habitats. It is home to **70** large mammal species, including **lions**, **giraffes**, and **wildebeest**, and **500 bird** species. It is also the region where some of the oldest fossils of our human ancestors have been found.

.....The fossils found in the Serengeti suggest that humans first evolved here.

MIGRATIONS

During the wet season, food is abundant, but dry seasons bring drought and water shortages. This forces the **huge herds** of **plant-eating** animals to migrate to wetter areas where the rains are still falling.

Every year in **East Africa**, a huge herd containing **1.5 million wildebeest, 200,000 zebras,** and thousands of antelope migrate in search of food and water.

Crocodiles lie in wait for the migrating wildebeest.

During their migration, wildebeest must cross crocodile-infested rivers.

SAVING WATER

Many plants in tropical grasslands are **xerophytic**, which means that they are adapted to cope with periods when **little** or **no** rain falls. For example, **acacia** trees have small, waxy leaves that minimize water loss and thorns to protect them from plant-eating animals.

Baobab trees store water in their trunks and have thick bark to protect them from grassland fires.

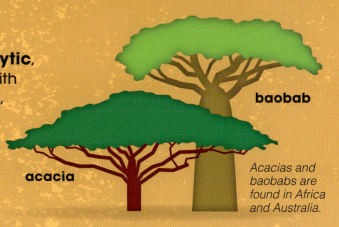

acacia baobab

Acacias and baobabs are found in Africa and Australia.

Australian tropical grasslands are home to many large animals, including the **red kangaroo** and the **emu**, both of which can stand up to **6.5 feet (2 m)** tall.

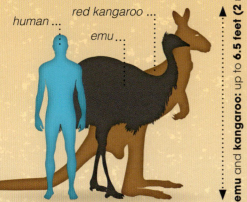

human... red kangaroo... emu...

emu and kangaroo: up to 6.5 feet (2 m)

The great wildebeest migration has been called one of the

SEVEN NEW WONDERS OF THE WORLD.

This annual event happens between the Serengeti National Park in Tanzania and the Maasai Mara National Reserve in Kenya.

RIVERS AND WETLANDS

As rain falls on Earth's surface, it collects to form streams and rivers that merge and flow into lakes, swamps, and other wetland areas. This fresh water and the nutrients carried in it create habitats that teem with life.

MIGHTY RIVER

At almost **4,000 miles (6,400 km)** long, the **Amazon** is the second-longest river in the world, but it is by far the largest in terms of volume of water. It drains a basin that covers **over 1 million square miles (2.7 million sq km)**. The Amazon carries about **20 percent** of all the water that runs off Earth's surface.

During the wet season, the Amazon swells to more than three times its size, covering an area of more than **13,500 square miles (35,000 sq km)** and flooding the surrounding land.

Amazon Basin.

Rio Negro

Amazon

Many other large rivers flow into the Amazon, including the Rio Negro, the seventh largest river in the world by volume.

EVERGLADES

The Everglades is a large area of tropical wetlands in south Florida and includes a mix of **fresh** and **saltwater** areas. It is home to more than **200,000 alligators**, which can grow more than **13 feet (4 m) long**. They hunt other **reptiles**, **birds,** and **mammals**, but luckily for us they mostly avoid humans.

It has recently been discovered that, as well as eating meat, alligators like to munch on a variety of fruits.

Although they are easily capable of killing a human, alligator attacks in the Everglades are rare.

INLAND DELTA

The **Okavango Delta** is a huge inland delta in **Botswana**, Africa. This region covers about **5,800 square miles (15,000 sq km)** and is flat, only varying in height by about **6.5 feet (2 m)**. Every year, water flows into the area, flooding it. Large animals, such as **elephants and zebra**, come to the delta to feed on the plants that grow there. Predators, such as **lions**, **cheetahs**, and **crocodiles**, lie in wait for them.

Botswana has the largest elephant population in Africa, with more than **135,000** Individuals.

INTO THE DEEP

Great Slave Lake, **Canada: 614 m (2014 ft)**

Crater Lake, **USA: 594 m (1950 ft)**

Loch Ness, **Scotland: 227 m (745 ft)**

Lake Baikal, **Russia: 1,620 m (5,315 ft)**

DEPTH IN METERS

500 meters

1,000 meters

1,500 meters

2,000 meters

Burj Khalifa, Dubai, UAE: 830 m (2,723 ft) to tip

DEEPEST LAKE

Lake Baikal in Russia is the **largest** freshwater lake in the world and the **deepest** continental body of water. Plunging to a depth of **5,315 feet (1,620 m)**, it is deep enough to hold nearly two **Burj Khalifa skyscrapers** on top of each other!

Lake Baikal formed **30 million** years ago from a rift valley, where two continental plates moved apart. It holds about **20 percent** of the world's surface fresh water, which is more than all of the North American **Great Lakes** combined.

More than **80 percent** of the animals that live in Lake Baikal, such as the **Baikal seal** and the **Baikal oilfish**, are found nowhere else.

The Baikal seal is one of the smallest seals in the world, growing up to 5 feet (1.5 m) long.

The Baikal oilfish is the main source of food for the Baikal seal. It is very hard to catch, so humans do not generally eat it.

DESERTS

Deserts are the driest places on the planet, but don't think they're all scorching hot, sand-covered habitats. Some are stoney wastelands, while others are found at the coldest places on Earth. The plants and animals that live here need special adaptations to cope with the harsh conditions.

DRY PLACES

Deserts are places that receive less than about **10 inches (250 mm)** of precipitation in a year. Temperatures vary from desert to desert, reaching above **122°F (50°C)** or plunging well below **freezing**.

HOT DESERTS
The largest **hot** desert is the **Sahara** in Africa. it covers about **3.5 million square miles (9 million sq km)**.

Across the whole world, about **2.5 MILLION SQUARE FEET (230,000 SQ M)** of land is turning to desert (a process called desertification) every single minute.

COLD DESERTS
The largest **cold** desert (and the largest desert of any kind) is **Antarctica**, which covers about **5.4 million square miles (14 million sq km)**.

Antarctica is the coldest, windiest, highest, and driest continent on **EARTH.**

ATACAMA

The **Atacama Desert** in Chile, South America, is formed in a rain shadow. Warm air blowing in from the **Pacific Ocean** contains plenty of water. As the air hits the Andes Mountains, it is **forced up** where it **cools**. As it gets **colder**, it **can't** hold on to the **water**, which falls as rain. The now dry air continues over the mountains, creating a dry rain shadow area on the other side.

The Atacama is the driest warm desert on Earth. Average rainfall is about **0.6 inch (15 mm)** a year.

Soil samples from the Atacama Desert are very similar to samples collected on **MARS.**

EXTREME SURVIVORS

Few animals can survive in the Atacama Desert. The **Chilean mouse opossum** is active mainly around dusk, when temperatures are falling.

Chilean mouse opossum

DESERT PLANTS

Cactuses are plants that are specially adapted to desert conditions. The thick succulent stems **hold on to water**. Their spines are modified leaves. They help to keep the plant cool by producing thousands of tiny shadows that protect it from the intense glare of the sun.

25

Cactuses range in size from just 0.4 inch (1 cm) tall to nearly 66 feet (20 m) in height.

DESERT ANIMALS

When animals find water in a desert, they make the most of it. A camel can drink up **to 53 gallons (200 l)** of water in three minutes. It can then go up to **10 days** without drinking at all.

By storing fat in its hump, a camel will stay cooler than if it had a thin layer of fat all around its body.

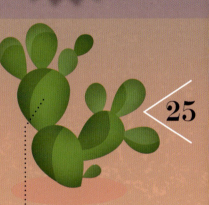

EATING DUNG

Dung beetles do not drink at all. They get all the water they need from the animal poop they eat.

Dung beetles roll balls of dung by pushing them with their hind legs.

A **Spencer's burrowing frog** survives in the **Australian** desert by **sleeping** under the sand. It stays there until **rains arrive**, at which point it **awakens** and climbs to the surface to feed and to mate.

Spencer's burrowing frog

MOUNTAINS

As mountains rise high into the air, conditions and climate change, as does the habitat. This creates distinct bands of habitats, each with their own types of plant and animal life.

CLIMATE ZONES

Mountains may have some or all of the below climate zones, each forming a distinct habitat with its own flora and fauna.

snow line .... very few things grow or live above this altitude
nival zone .... only mosses and lichens grow here
alpine zone .... consists of grass meadows
treeline .... uppermost limit where trees grow
subalpine zone .... contains coniferous forests
montane zone .... a mix of deciduous and coniferous forests
foothills zone .... consists of deciduous forests

−5°F

Temperatures drop by up to **5°F** for every **1,000 feet (300 m)** climbed.

KILIMANJARO

Found south of the equator, Mount Kilimanjaro is the **highest mountain in Africa**. It is **19,340 feet (5,895 m)** tall. As you climb the mountain, you pass through different habitats, from the baking hot bushland at its base to the permanent ice cap above 16,400 feet (5,000 m).

19,340 feet (5,895 m)

snow line — permanent snow – no plants or large animals

16,400 feet (5,000 m)

nival zone — moss and lichen .... insects and spiders

13,120 feet (4,000 m)

alpine zone — grasses and heather .... shrews

9,190 feet (2,800 m)

montane zone — dense jungle .... colobus monkeys

5,900 feet (1,800 m)

foothills zone — coffee .... humans

2,620 feet (800 m)

MOUNTAIN ANIMALS

Animals that live on mountains have to cross difficult terrain. As a result, large mountain creatures, such as the **chamois** and **mountain sheep**, are extremely agile and sure-footed.

Mountain animals also have to cope with extreme cold. Many of them, including **mountain leopards**, **llamas**, and **chinchillas**, have developed thick coats to beat the chill.

People use llama wool for clothing because it is light, warm and water-repellent.

The **RINGS** on a mountain goat's horns can tell you its age in years, which is the number of rings minus one!

The chamois is a species of goat-antelope found in the European Alps. Quick and sure-footed, it's fast on the uneven rocky terrain.

bearded vulture

Snow leopards have huge paws that act as snowshoes to keep them from sinking into the snow.

BONE COLLECTOR

The **bearded vulture** lives in the mountains of Europe, Asia, and Africa. It feeds almost entirely on the **bones** of dead animals, taking its **nutrients** from the bone marrow. Bearded vultures have been seen on **Mount Everest** at altitudes above **23,00 feet (7,000 m)**.

HUMAN IMPACT

People moving into highland areas to settle and farm land have reduced the size of wild habitats and the numbers of animals that live there. In the mountains of Central Asia, there are now as few as **4,000 snow leopards** left in the wild.

A bearded vulture's stomach contains extra-strong acid to break down bone.

TUNDRA AND THE POLES

The extreme north and south of the planet are covered in cold, frozen regions. Temperatures are so low that the ground is either permanently frozen all-year round, restricting plant life, or covered in thick layers of ice and snow, stopping plant life from growing at all.

THE POLES

The ice sheet covering Antarctica is nearly **15,750 feet (4,800 m)** deep at its thickest. About **95 percent** of the continent is covered with ice.

Earth is tilted in its orbit, which means that the regions around the poles experience **24 hours** of sunlight a day during the height of summer, and **24 hours** of **darkness** in the depths of winter.

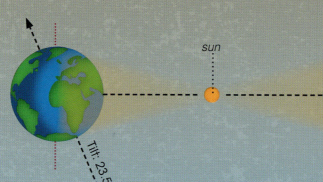

DECEMBER
- winter in the Northern Hemisphere
- summer in the Southern Hemisphere

JUNE
- summer in the Northern Hemisphere
- winter in the Southern Hemisphere

APEX PREDATOR

In the Arctic, the polar bear is the apex (top) predator. To cope with the extreme cold, **polar bears** have:

- **fur** on the soles of their feet to insulate them against the ice.
- **large feet** to grip on the ice and swim through the water.
- **sharp teeth** and **claws** to catch prey quickly.
- **thick fur** to insulate the body and camouflage the animal against the snow.
- **thick layers** of **fat**, or **blubber**, for warmth.

Polar bears are champion swimmers, able to cover more than **62 MILES (100 KM)** without stopping.

DIGGING DOWN

In the long winter, most of the ground is covered with deep snow. Grazing animals have to dig through the snow to find food.

TUNDRA

Tundra comes from the Finnish word *tuntria*, meaning "treeless land."

The Arctic tundra in the far north is covered in snow for about eight months each year.

During winter, caribou dig lichen out from under the snow for food.

PERMAFROST

Below the surface of the tundra regions is a thick layer of permanently frozen soil, called **permafrost**.

At its deepest, this permafrost can reach down to **4,760 feet (1,450 m)**. The frozen soil stops plants with deep roots from growing and prevents animals digging deep burrows for shelter.

SUMMER

In summer months, rising temperatures in the tundra cause the very top layer of the soil to thaw, plants to **grow** and **bloom** and insects to hatch. This eruption of life attracts migrating animals, including flocks of birds, such as **snow geese**.

The plants that bloom during summer in the Arctic tundra include bearberries, cushion plants, and the Arctic willow.

Snow geese arrive in the Arctic tundra every spring. They nest and raise young before flying south for the winter.

GLOSSARY

ALGAE
Tiny plants that grow in water and lack stems, roots, or leaves.

ALGAL BLOOM
The rapid growth in the number of tiny marine organisms. Some of these blooms are so big that they can be seen from space.

AMPHIBIOUS
Able to live both on land and in water.

BARK
The tough outer covering of a tree. It protects the inner parts of the trunk and branches, reducing water loss and preventing damage caused by animals.

CRUSTACEANS
A type of animal that has a hard outer shell and several pairs of legs. They include crabs.

DELTA
A triangle-shaped area of sand and soil deposited at the mouth of some large rivers.

DESERT
The name given to a region that receives less than 10 inches (250 mm) of precipitation (rain, snow, or hail) in a year. Deserts can be hot, such as the Sahara, or cold, such as Antarctica.

EQUATOR
An imaginary circle around Earth halfway between the North Pole and the South Pole.

EROSION
The gradual wearing away of soil or Earth's surface by wind, rain, or another natural matter.

HABITAT
This is the natural environment in which a living thing lives.

HIBERNATION
A sleep-like state that many animals enter during cold periods. Their body actions slow down, saving energy when food and water may be in short supply.

HYDROTHERMAL VENTS
Holes in the seabed through which gushes super-hot water that is rich in minerals.

INVERTEBRATE
A type of animal that does not have a backbone. Invertebrates include insects and soft-bodied animals, such as octopuses.

MAMMAL
A type of warm-blooded animal that has a body covered with hair and that produces milk to feed its young.

MIGRATION
The regular movement of animals from one place to another, usually in search of food, water, or a place to give birth.

NUTRIENTS
Substances found that help animals, people, and plants live and grow.

ORGANISM
A living thing, such as an animal, plant, or bacteria.

OXYGEN
A colorless, odorless gas that is used by all living things to produce energy.

PAMPAS
A large area of grassland found in South America.

PHOTOSYNTHESIS
The process by which plants use sunlight, carbon dioxide, and water to produce sugars and release oxygen into the air.

POLES
The most northern and southern points on Earth are known as the North Pole and the South Pole (the poles).

PRAIRIE
A large area of grassland found in North America.

RAIN FOREST
A forested region that receives a lot of rain all year round.

SEDIMENT
Material carried by wind or water that settles on the sea- or riverbed or the surface of the land.

SPECIES
A group of living things that look and behave in the same way and produce fertile young that can have young of their own.

STEPPE
A large area of grassland that stretches from Eastern Europe and across Asia.

TAIGA
The name given to a large band of forest that stretches across northern parts of Asia, Europe, and North America.

TEMPERATE
The name given to parts of the world that lie nearer to the poles than the tropical regions.

TROPICAL
The name given to parts of the world that lie near the equator.

TUNDRA
Huge, treeless plains found in the Arctic regions of North America, Europe, and Asia.

INDEX

acacia tree 21
algae 6
alligator 22
Amazon Rain Forest 17
Amazon River 22
Antarctica 24, 28
antelope 20
Arctic 28–29
Atacama Desert 25

bacteria 7
Baikal, Lake 23
baobab tree 21
bearded vulture 27
bears 13, 15, 28
bison 19
black bear 15
blue whale 7
boreal forests 12–13
brown bear 13
buffalo 19

cactuses 25
camels 25
caribou 13, 29
Challenger Deep 6
chlorophyll 14
chamois 27
clams 11
climate change 11
continental shelf 6
coral 10–11
crocodiles 20

deciduous trees 14
dolphins 10
dung beetles 25

elephants 23
emu 21
epiphytes 17
Everglades 22
evergreen trees 12, 14

fringe-toed lizard 5
Fundy, Bay of 8
Furnace Creek 5

giant oarfish 7
giant redwoods 17
giant squid 7
Great Barrier Reef 10
gulls 10

hermit crab 8
hibernation 13
hoolock gibbon 5
humphead wrasse 11
hydrothermal vents 7

jellyfish 10

kelp 9
Kilimanjaro 26

leaf litter 14
limpets 9
llama 27

manatees 9
mangrove swamps 9
McMurdo Dry Valleys 5
Meghalaya 5
migration 13, 20, 21
mudskippers 9

oak tree 15
Okavango Delta 23
orchids 17
oriole 15

pampas 18
permafrost 29
photosynthesis 16
plankton 6
polar bears 28
prairie dog 19

prairies 18, 19

rays 10
red kangaroo 21
reindeer 13
Rio Negro 22
rock pools 8

Sahara 24
salamander 15
sea anemones 8
seagrass 9
seasons 14, 18, 20
sea worms 11
Serengeti 20, 21
shoreline 6, 8–9
snow geese 29
snow leopard 27
Spencer's burrowing frog 25
spiders 15
sponges 11
starfish 8
steppe 18

taiga 12–13
tawny owl 15
temperate forests 14–15, 17
Teresensis' bromeliad treefrog 17
tides 8
tube worms 7
tundra 29
turtles 11

Vostok Station 5

whale shark 7, 11
wildebeest 20, 21
wildfires 19
wolves 13

zebra 20